"The Ride of the Valkyries"
and Other Highlights from The Ring

in Full Score

Richard Wagner

DOVER PUBLICATIONS, INC.
Mineola, New York

Bibliographical Note

This Dover edition, first published in 1996, is a new compilation of six scores originally published separately. B. Schott's Söhne, Mainz, originally published *Der Ritt der Walküren aus dem Musik-Drama Die Walküre von R. Wagner / für Orchester zum Conzertvortrag eingerichtet*, edition No. 22139, n.d.; and *Trauermarsch beim Tode Siegfried's aus dem Musik-Drama Götterdämmerung / für grosses Orchester von Richard Wagner*, edition No. 21998, n.d. The other scores in this compilation were originally published in early authoritative editions, n.d., including: *Einzug der Götter in Walhall* (from *Das Rheingold*); *Wotans Abschied und Feuerzauber* (from *Die Walküre*); *Waldweben* (from *Siegfried*); and *Siegfrieds Rheinfahrt* (from *Götterdämmerung*), transcribed by Engelbert Humperdinck.

The Dover edition adds lists of contents and instrumentation, a glossary of German terms and English translations of four footnotes. A few errors in the scores have been corrected, including incorrect pitches in "Wotan's Farewell," p. 123, and missing accidentals throughout the timpani part of that work.

We are grateful to the Duke University Music Library for the loan of several scores.

International Standard Book Number: 0-486-29375-0

Manufactured in the United States of America
Dover Publications, Inc., 31 East 2nd Street, Mineola, N.Y. 11501

Contents

Glossary of German Terms　　　　*vii*

Entry of the Gods into Valhalla . . . . 　1
"Einzug der Götter in Walhall" from *Das Rheingold*
(completed 1854)

The Ride of the Valkyries . . . . 　41
"Der Ritt der Walküren" from *Die Walküre*
(completed 1856)

Wotan's Farewell and Magic Fire Music . . . . 　89
"Wotans Abschied und Feuerzauber" from *Die Walküre*
(completed 1856)

Forest Murmurs . . . . 　159
"Waldweben" from *Siegfried*
(completed 1869)

Siegfried's Rhine Journey . . . . 　201
"Siegfrieds Rheinfahrt" from *Götterdämmerung*
(completed 1874)

Siegfried's Funeral Music . . . . 　225
"Trauermarsch beim Tode Siegfried's" from *Götterdämmerung*
(completed 1874)

Glossary of German Terms

abnehmend, diminishing
Abth[eilung], section
alle, all (*tutti*)
As u. Es, Des (etc.), A-flat and E-flat, D-flat (etc.) (timpani tunings)
ausdrucksv[oll], expressively

B, B-flat
beide, both
betont, accented
bewegt, moving, agitated
B nach H stimmen, B-flat to B-natural (timpani tuning)
Bog[en], bowed (*arco*)

Cis, C-sharp

d[ie] 1ᵉ (3ᵉ, etc.), the first (third, etc.) [player of the section]
Des, D-flat
Doppelgriff, doublestop
dritte Scene, third scene
durch Flag[eolet], using harmonics

eine, one
einer allein, one solo
erste[n], first, principal
ersterbend, dying away
Es, E-flat
E u. H, Fis u. H (etc.), E and B, F-sharp and B (etc.) (timpani tunings)
etwas belebter, somewhat animated
etwas langsamer, somewhat slower
etwas zurückhaltend, slightly held back

feierlich, solemnly
Fis, F-sharp

gebunden, connected (*legato*)
gestossen, driving forward
geth[eilt], get., divided (*divisi*)
gleichmäßig geteilt = sempre divisi
gut betont, well accented
gut gehalten, quite steady, well controlled

H, B-natural
Hälfte, half [of the section]
hell, brightly
hoch F nach Es stimmen (etc.), high F to E-flat (timpani tuning)

immer, always, steadily
immer sehr kräftig, always very forceful
immer stark, always strong
in dem selben Zeitmaß, in the same tempo
in Ermangelung der 1ᵉⁿ gr. Fl., in the absence of the 1st flute
in Es, Ges (etc.), [tuned to] E-flat, G-flat (etc.) (timpani)

in mässiger Stärke, with moderate force
in tief F (etc.), [tuned to] low F (timpani)

kräftig, forceful

lange, long
langsam, slow
lebhaft, lively
leidenschaftlich, passionately

mässig [mäßig], moderate
mässig bewegt, moderately agitated
mit Dämpfer, muted
mit Paukenschlägeln, with timpani sticks

nach C stimmen, [tune to] C (timpani)
natürlich, [play] naturally [in the usual way]
noch etwas zurückhaltend, still rather restrained
nur die Hälfte, half [of the section] only
nur 2 (3, etc.), only 2 (etc.) players

oder, or
offen, open (for brass)

Paar, Pr., P., pair
   ["1ˢ P.H." = lst pair (of trumpets) play the B-natural]
   ["2ˢ Pr. Cis" = 2nd pair (of timpani) tune to C-sharp]
Part(ie), part

rasch, quick
ruhig, calm

schnell, fast
sehr, very
   (modifies other words in this glossary)
sehr ruhig, ohne zu schleppen, very calm, without dragging

tief F nach G stimmen, [tune] low F to G (timpani)

u., und, and

verdoppelt, doubled
von hier an bedeutend abnehmend, from this point on diminishing significantly

weich, delicate, smooth, tender
wie entfernt, as from a distance

zart, subdued, gentle
ziemlich rasch, rather quick
zurückhaltend, holding back
zu 2 = a2
zus[ammen], together
zweite[n], second (of two or more instruments)

"The Ride of the Valkyries"
and Other Highlights from The Ring

Entry of the Gods into Valhalla

"Einzug der Götter in Walhall"

from *Das Rheingold*

(completed 1854)

Entry of the Gods into Valhalla

INSTRUMENTATION

2 Flutes [Flöten, Fl.]
2 Oboes [Hoboen, Hb.]
2 Clarinets [Clarinetten, Cl.]
2 Bassoons [Fagotte, Fag.]

4 Horns [Hörner, Hör.]
3 Trumpets [Trompeten, Tromp.]
3 Trombones [Posaunen, Pos.]
Bass Tuba [Bass-Tuba, Bs.Tub.]

Cymbals [Becken, Beck.]
Timpani [Pauken, Pauk.]

Harp [Harfe]

Violins 1, 2 [Violinen, Viol.]
Violas [Bratschen, Br.]
Cellos [Violoncelle, Vc.]
Basses [Contrabässe, CB.]

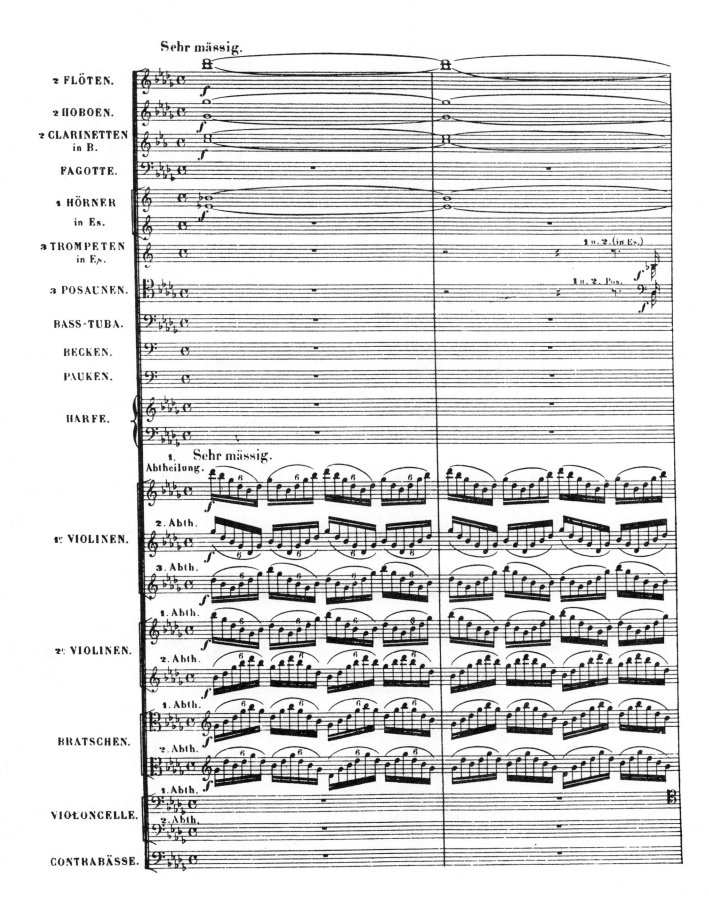

8   *Entry of the Gods into Valhalla*

12   Entry of the Gods into Valhalla

14   Entry of the Gods into Valhalla

18   Entry of the Gods into Valhalla

24   Entry of the Gods into Valhalla

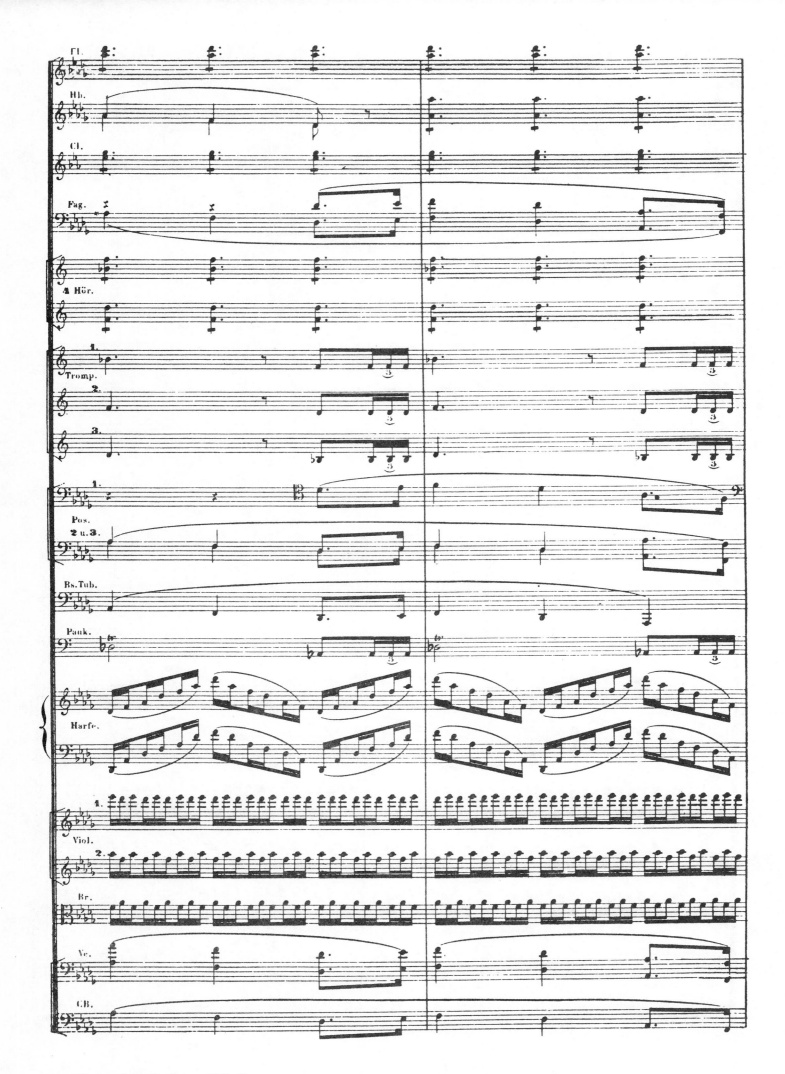

38   Entry of the Gods into Valhalla

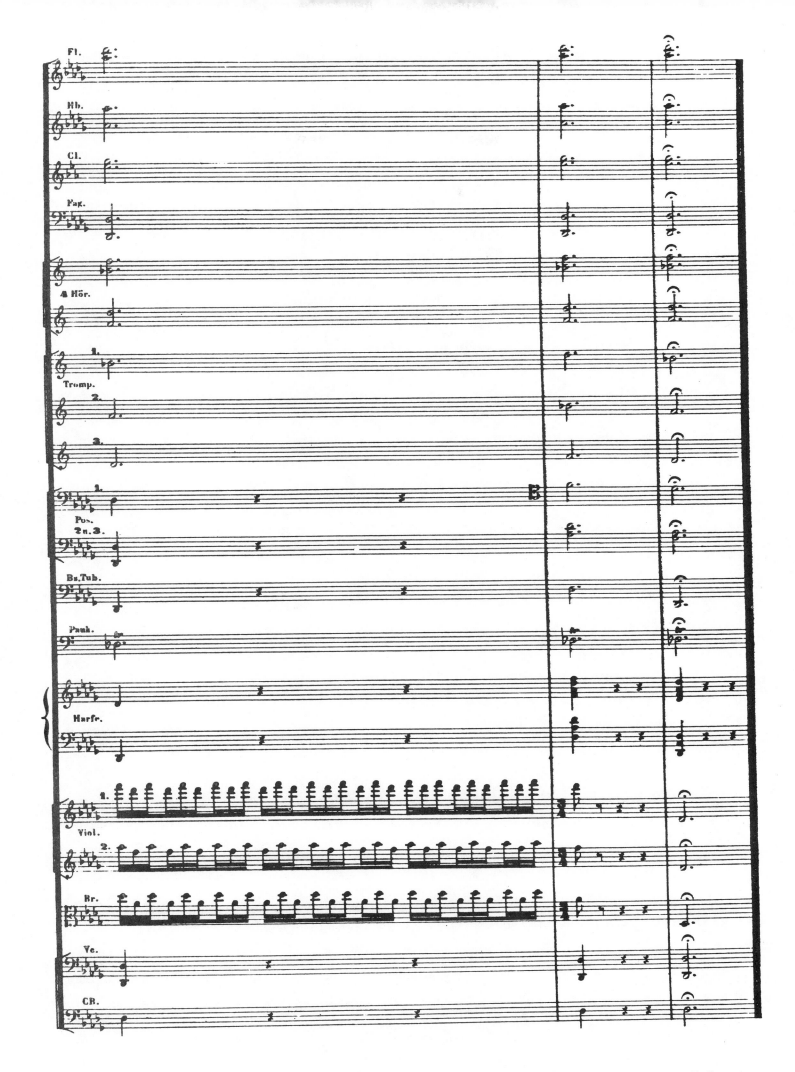

The Ride of the Valkyries

"Der Ritt der Walküren"

from *Die Walküre*

(completed 1856)

The Ride of the Valkyries
INSTRUMENTATION

2 Piccolos [kleine Flöten, kl. Fl.]
2 Flutes [grosse Flöten, gr. Fl.]
3 Oboes [Hoboen, Hob.]
English Horn [Engl. Horn (Hr.)]
3 Clarinets [Clarinetten, Cl.]
Bass Clarinet [Bass Clarinette, Bs.Cl.]
3 Bassoons [Fagotte, Fag.]

8 Horns [Hörner, Hör., Hr.]
3 Trumpets [Trompeten, Tromp.]
4 Trombones [Posaunen, Pos.]
Contrabass Tuba [Contrabass-Tuba, CB.Tub.]

Timpani [Pauken, Pauk.]

Percussion:
   Triangle [Triang(e)l]
   Cymbals [Becken, Beck.]
   Tenor Drum* [Rührtr(ommel)]

Violins 1, 2 [Violinen, Viol.]
Violas [Bratschen, Br.]
Cellos [Violoncelle, Vc.]
Basses [Contrabässe, CB.]

*A *kleine Trommel* (snare drum) is mistakenly named on the first score page.
The *Rührtrommel* (tenor drum) (see p. 65) is the correct instrument.

76   The Ride of the Valkyries

82   The Ride of the Valkyries

Wotan's Farewell
and Magic Fire Music
"Wotans Abschied und Feuerzauber"
from *Die Walküre*
(completed 1856)

*Wotan's Farewell
and Magic Fire Music*

INSTRUMENTATION

2 Flutes [Flöten, Fl.]
2 Oboes [Hoboen, Hb.]
2 Clarinets [Clarinetten, Cl.]
2 Bassoons [Fagotte, Fag.]

4 Horns [Hörner, Hör.]
2 Trumpets [Trompeten, Tromp.]
3 Trombones [Posaunen, Pos.]
Bass Tuba [Bass-Tuba, Bs.Tub.]

Timpani [Pauken, Pauk.]

Violins 1, 2 [Violinen, Viol.]
Violas [Bratschen, Br.]
Cellos [Violoncelle, Vc.]
Basses [Contrabässe, CB.]

126   Wotan's Farewell and Magic Fire Music

130   Wotan's Farewell and Magic Fire Music

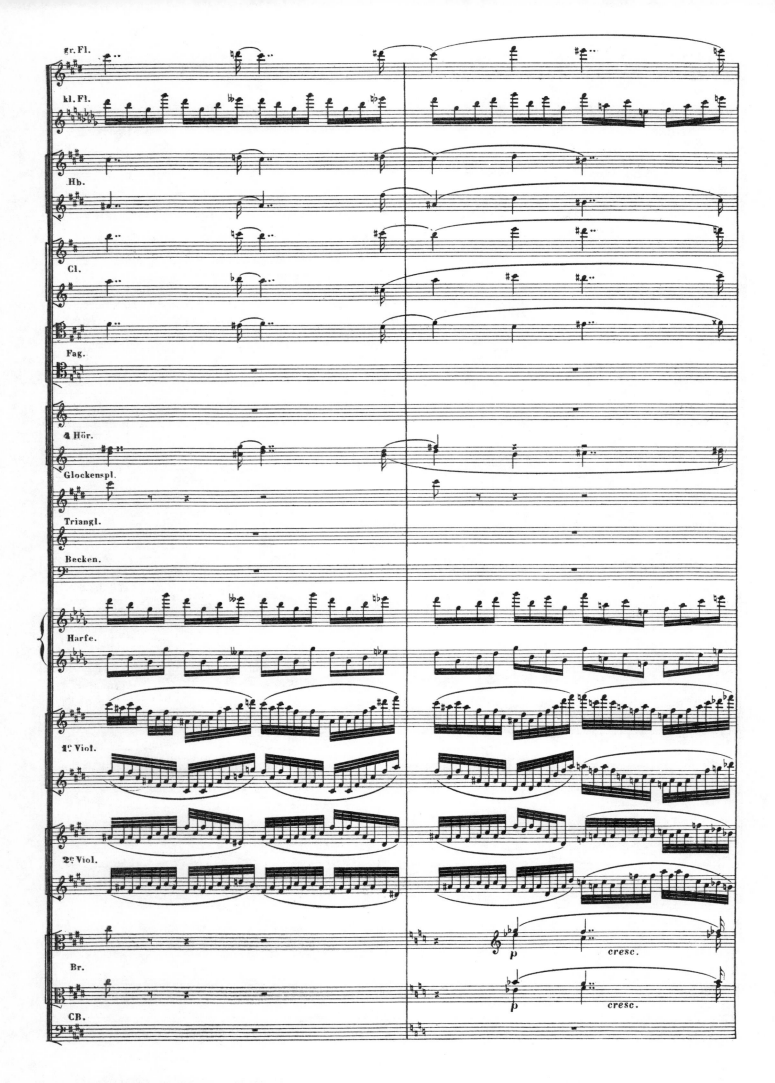

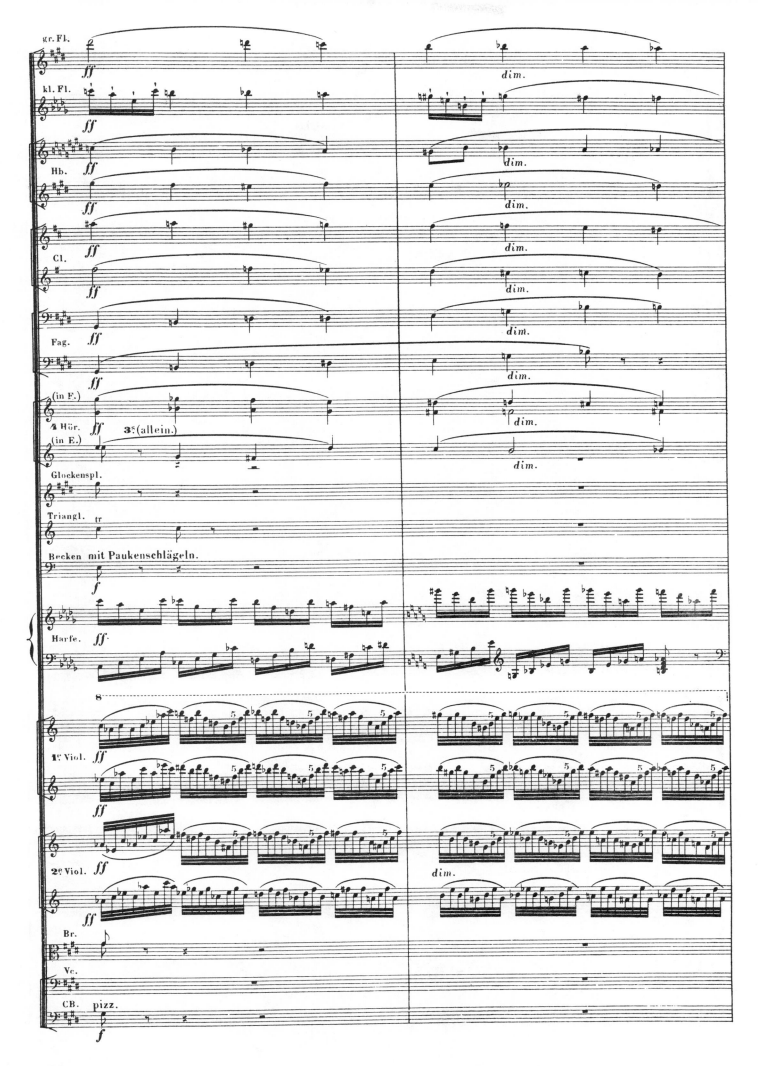

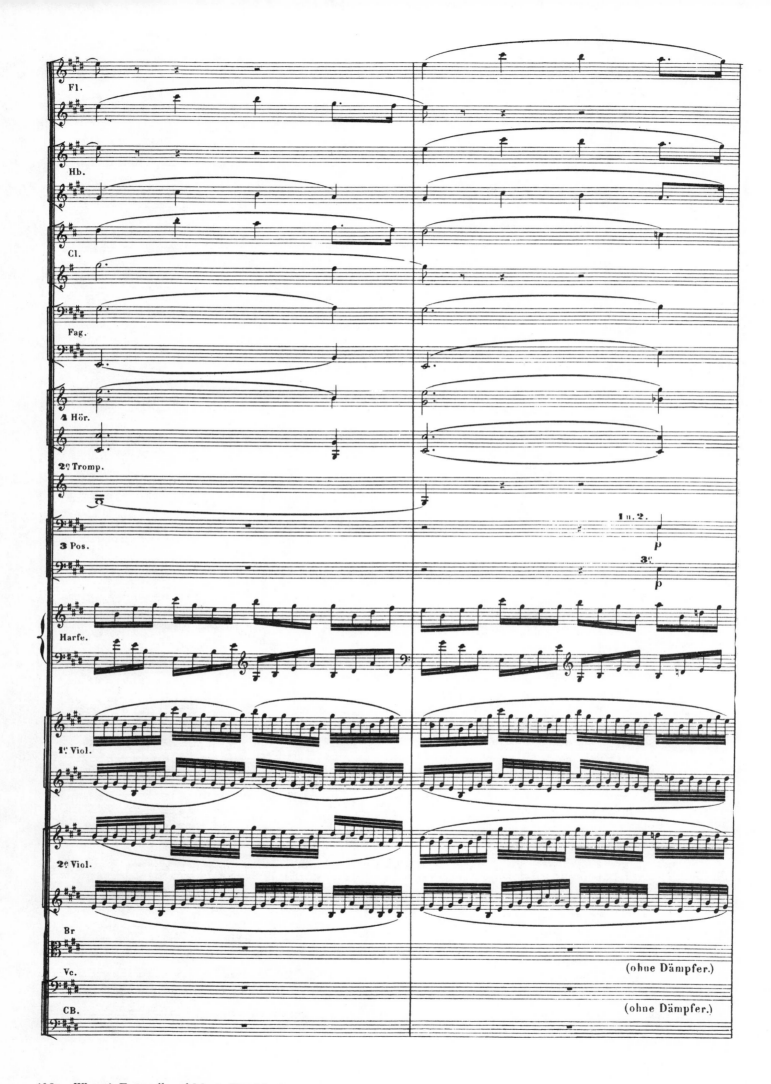

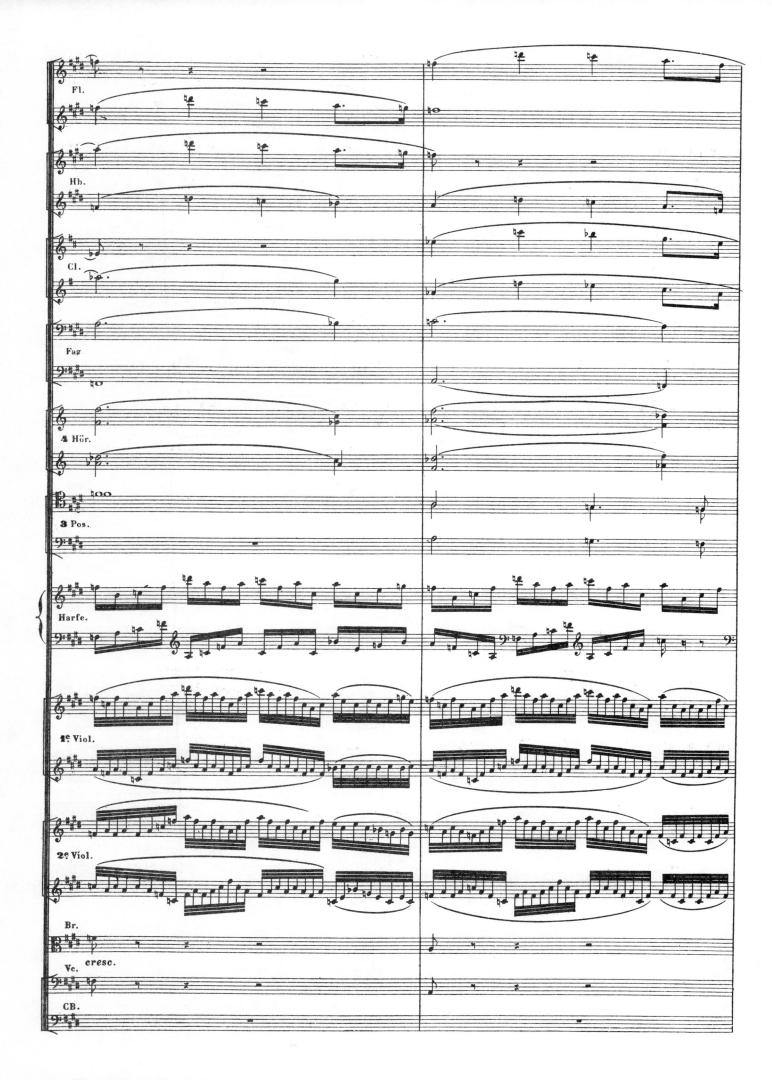

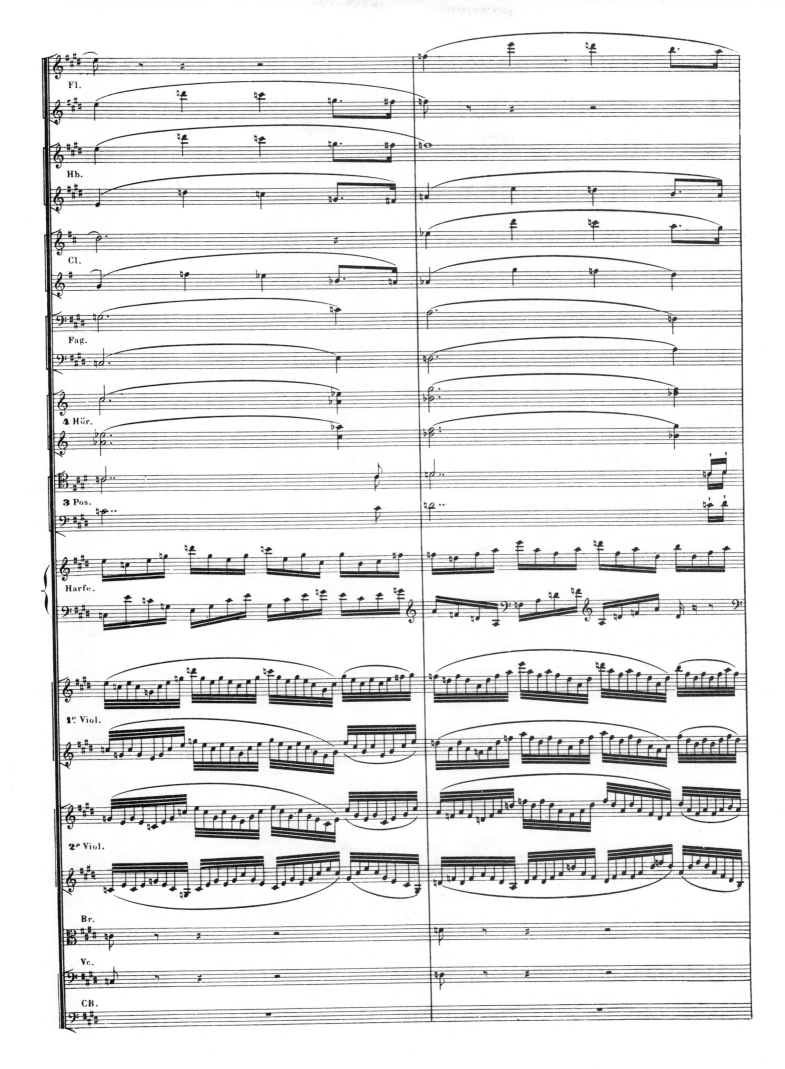

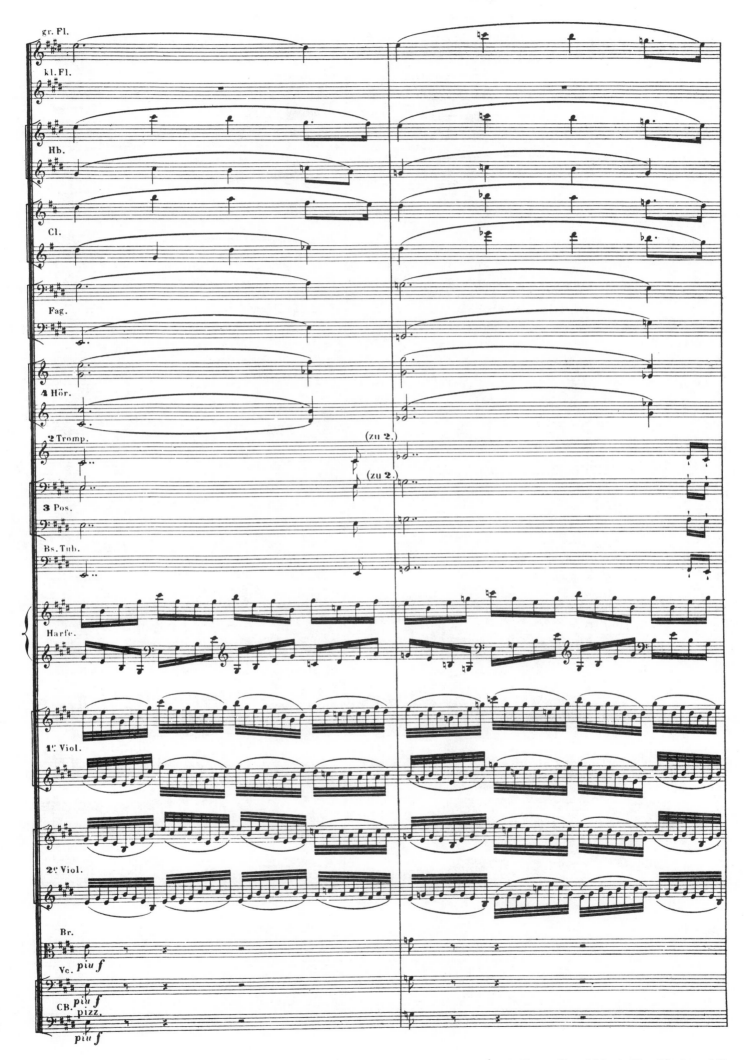

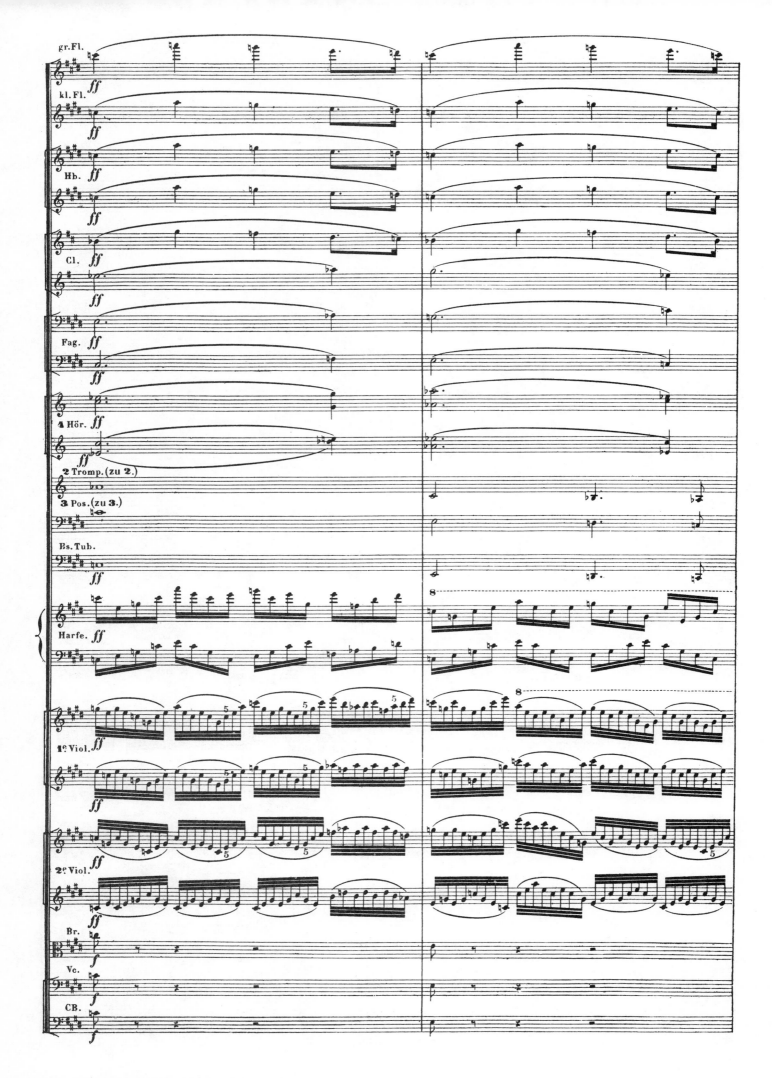

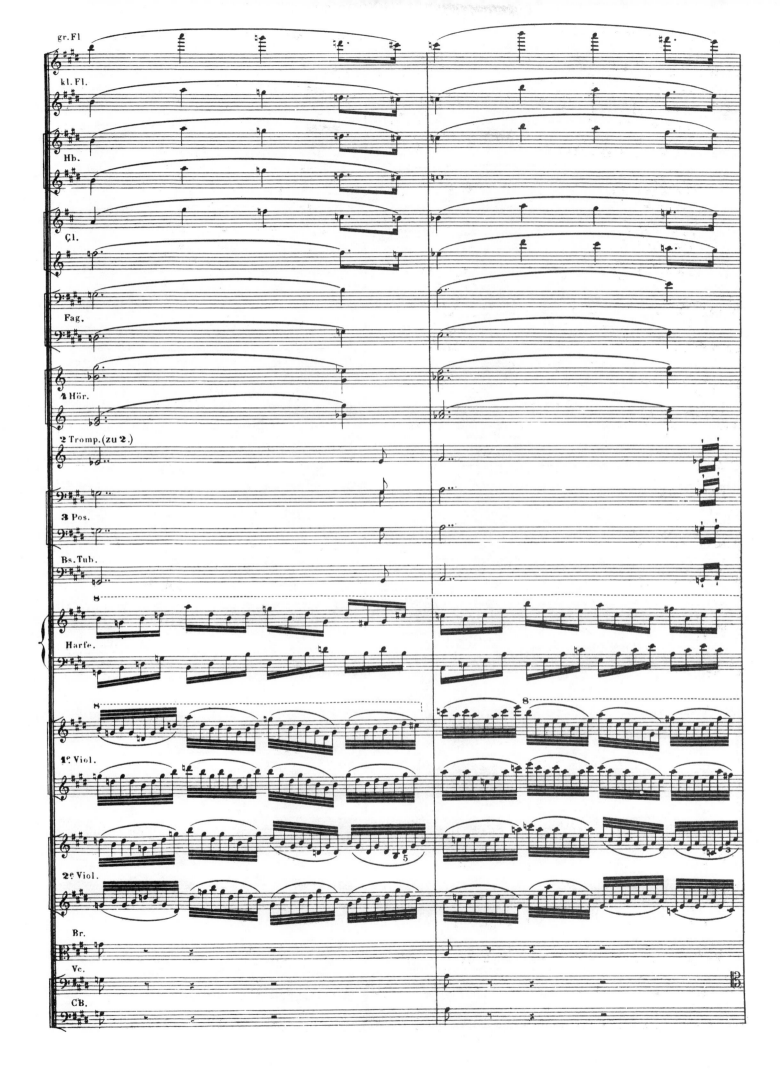

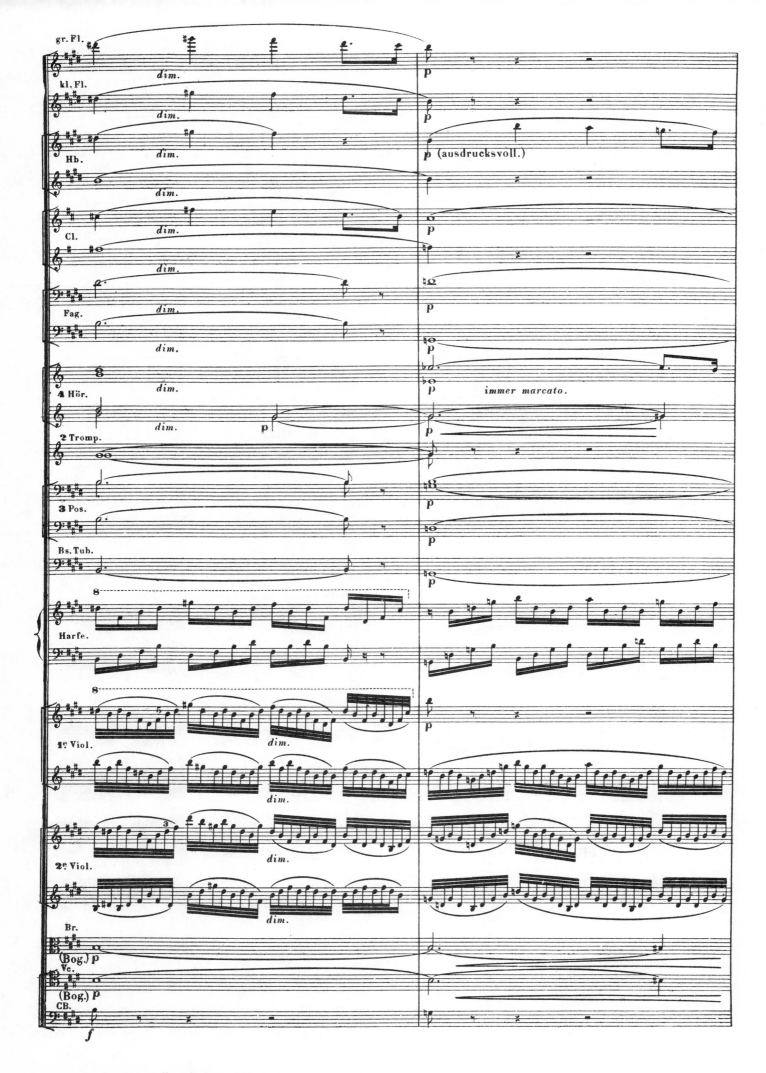

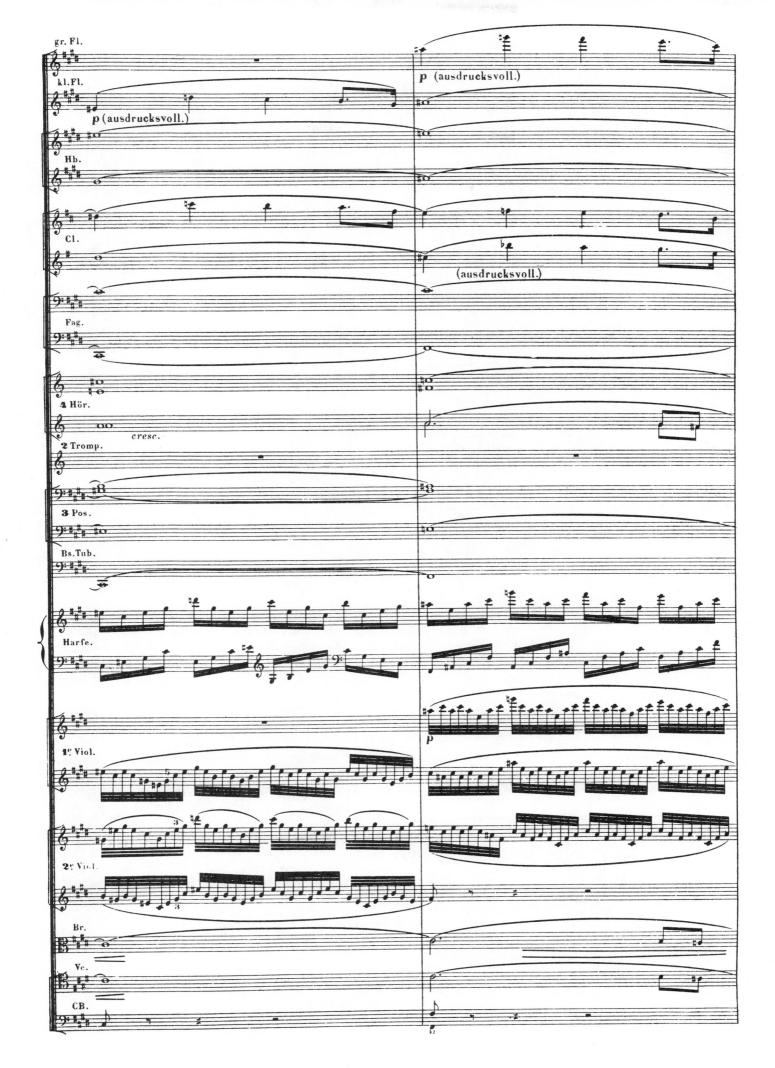

148   Wotan's Farewell and Magic Fire Music

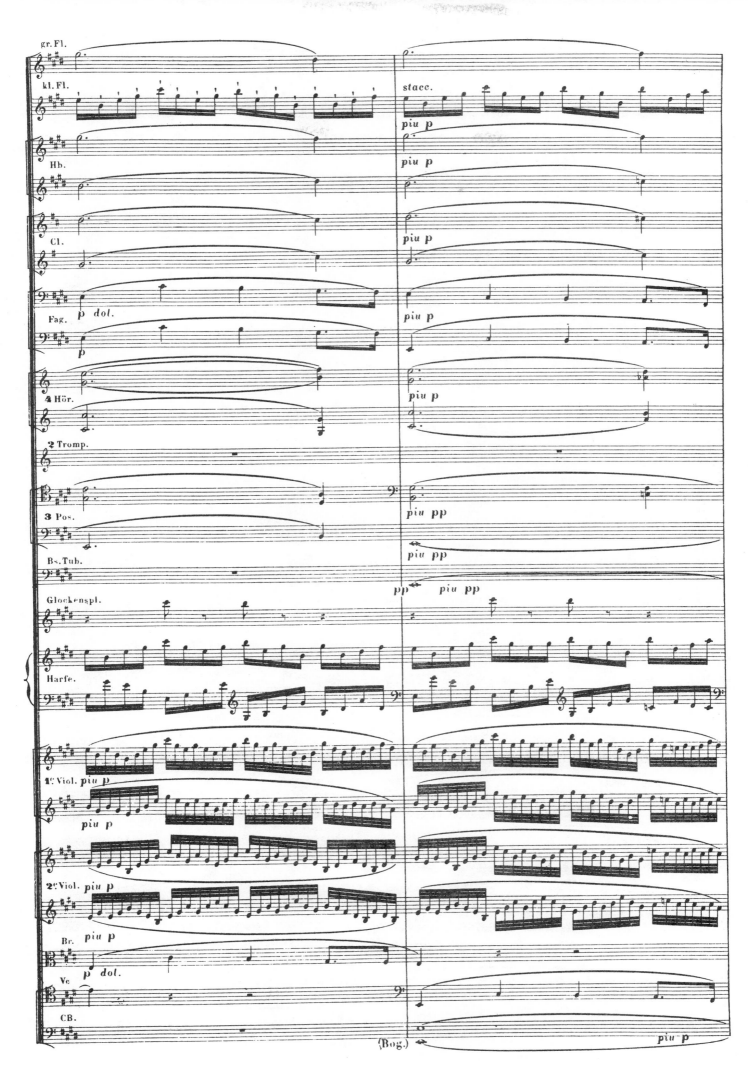

152   Wotan's Farewell and Magic Fire Music

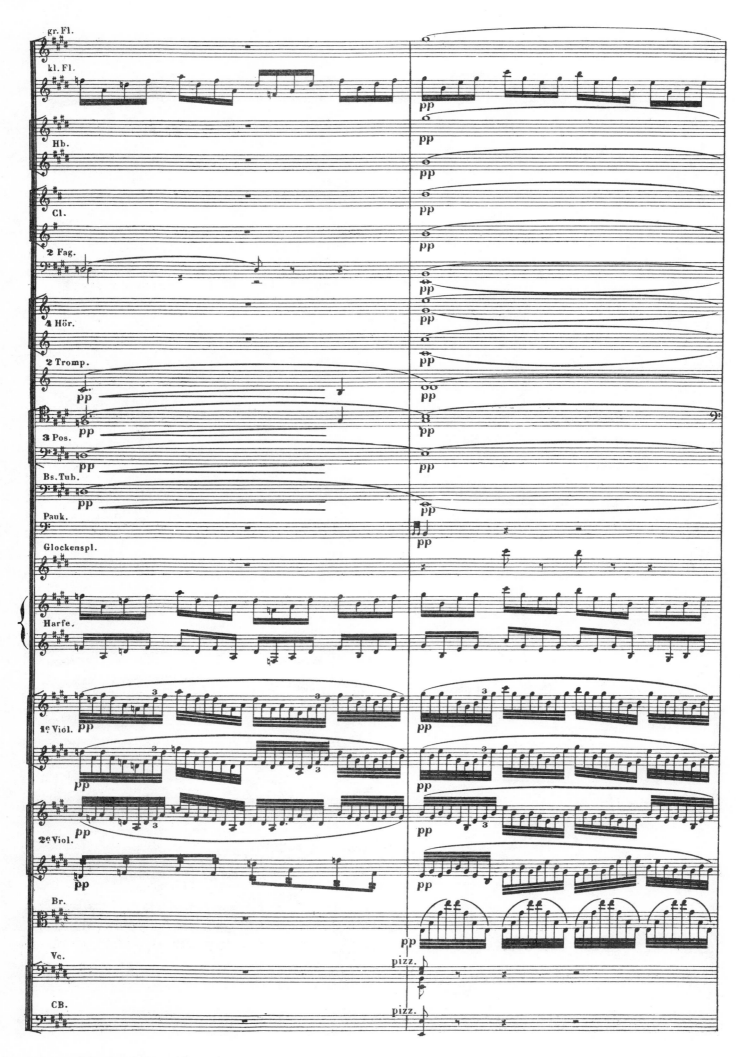

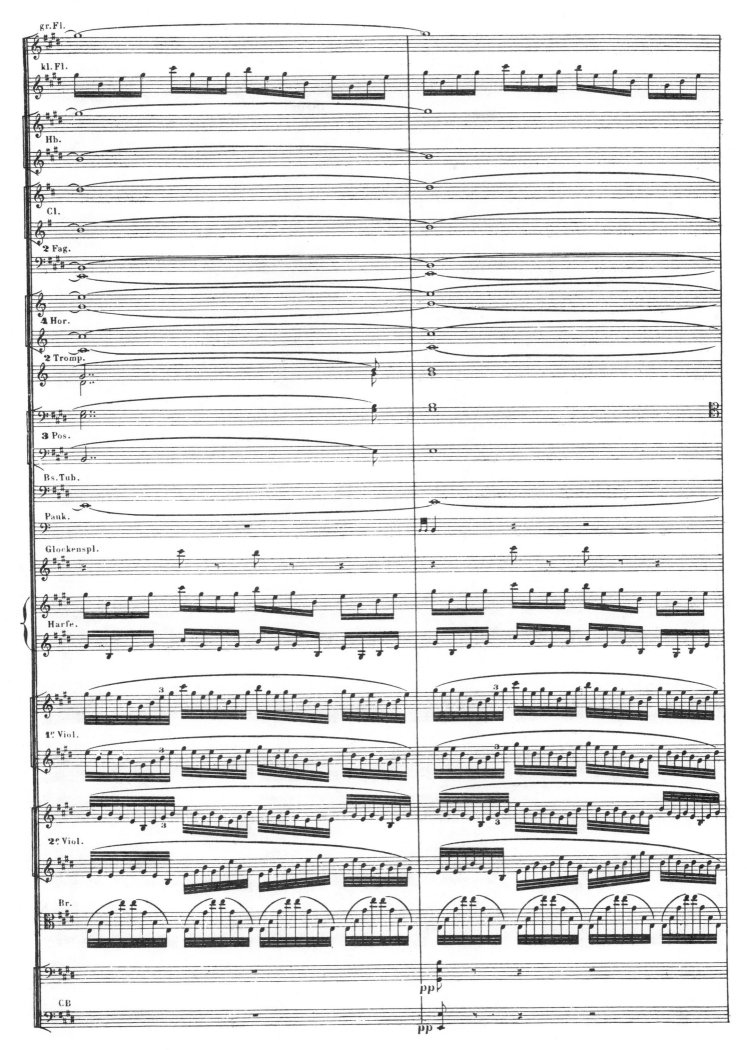

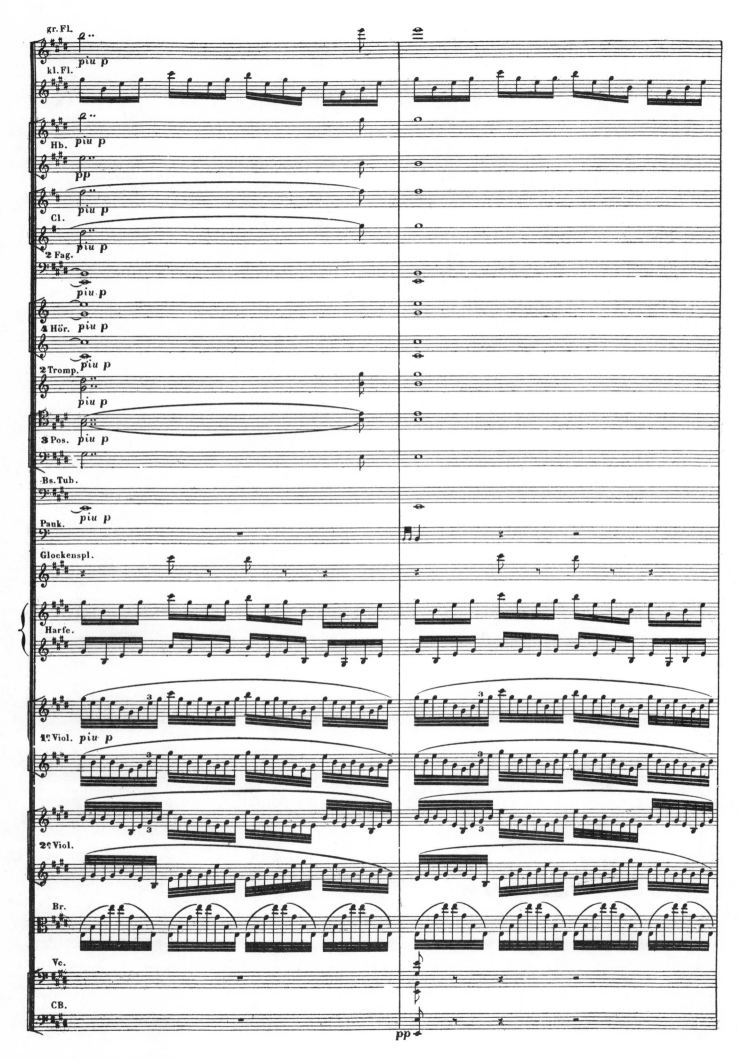

Forest Murmurs

"Waldweben"

from *Siegfried*

(completed 1869)

Forest Murmurs
INSTRUMENTATION

2 Flutes [Große Flöte, gr. Fl.]
   Flute 2 doubles Piccolo [Kleine Flöte, kl. Fl.]
2 Oboes [Hoboen, Hob.]
2 Clarinets [Klarinetten, Klar.]
2 Bassoons [Fagotte, Fag.]

4 Horns [Hörner, Hr.]
2 Trumpets [Trompeten, Trp.]
3 Trombones [Posaunen, Pos.]

Timpani [Pauken, Pauk.]

Percussion:
   Triangle [Triangel, Trgl.]
   Glockenspiel [Glockensp.]

Violins 1, 2 [Violinen, Viol.]
Violas [Bratschen, Br.]
Cellos [Violoncelle, Vcl.]
Basses [Kontrabässe, Kb.]

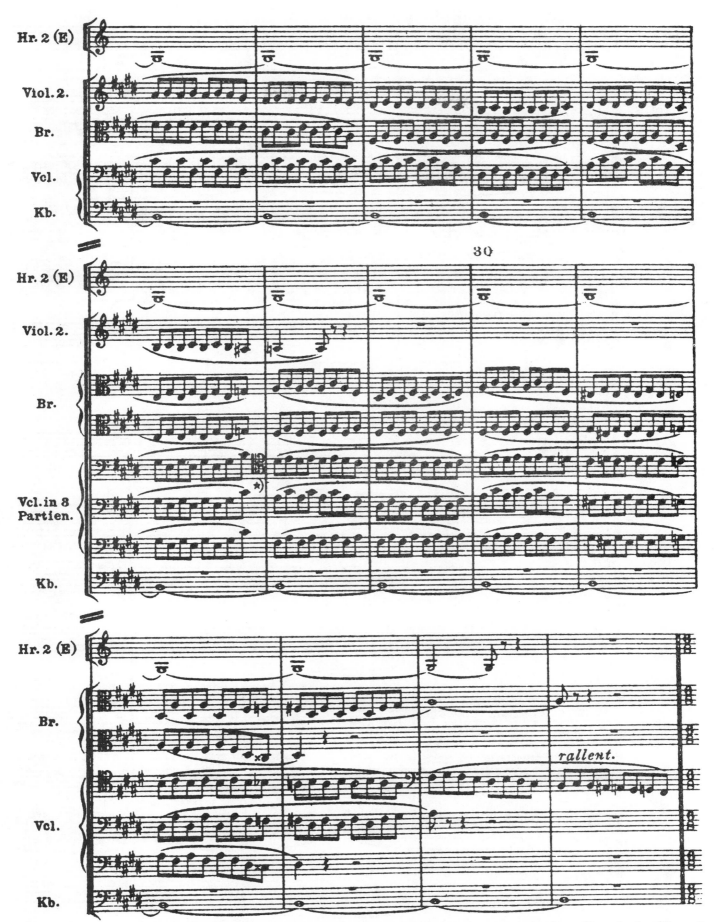

*) **Sind nicht genügend viel Violoncelli vorhanden, so bleiben die 2. u. 3. Partie derselben fort, während die erste Partie als Solo-Violoncell behandelt werden muß.**

[If there are not enough cellos available, the second and third parts are to be omitted, while the first part must be treated as a cello solo.]

*) (Die Dämpfer sind von den betreffenden Spielern nicht zugleich, sondern schnell nach einander abzunehmen!)

[The performers involved are not all to remove their mutes at the same time, but rather one after another in quick succession.]

*) 9 Achtel zu 6 der Begleitung, sodaß das letzte Viertel mit Punkt in Melodie und Begleitung zusammenfällt.

[9 eighths to 6 in the accompaniment, so that the melody and accompaniment come together on the last dotted quarter note.]

Siegfried's Rhine Journey

"Siegfrieds Rheinfahrt"

from *Götterdämmerung*

(completed 1874)

Orchestral transcription and last thirteen measures by

Engelbert Humperdinck

Siegfried's Rhine Journey

INSTRUMENTATION

Piccolo [Kleine Flöte, Kl. Fl.]
1 (or 2) Flutes [grosse Flöten, gr. Fl.]
2 Oboes [Hoboen, Hob.]
2 Clarinets [Clarinetten, Cl.]
4 Horns [Hörner, Hör.]
2 Bassoons [Fagotte, Fag.]

2 (or 3) Trumpets [Trompeten, Tromp.]
3 Trombones [Posaunen, Pos.]
Bass Tuba [Basstube, Bstub.]

2 (or 3) Timpani [Pauken, Pauk.]

Percussion:
    Glockenspiel (*ad lib.*) [Glockensp(ie)l]
    Triangle [Triang(e)l]
    Cymbals [Becken]

Harp [Harfe]

Violins 1, 2 [Violinen, Viol.]
Violas [Bratschen, Br.]
Cellos [Violoncelle, Vc.]
Basses [Contrabässe, Cb.]

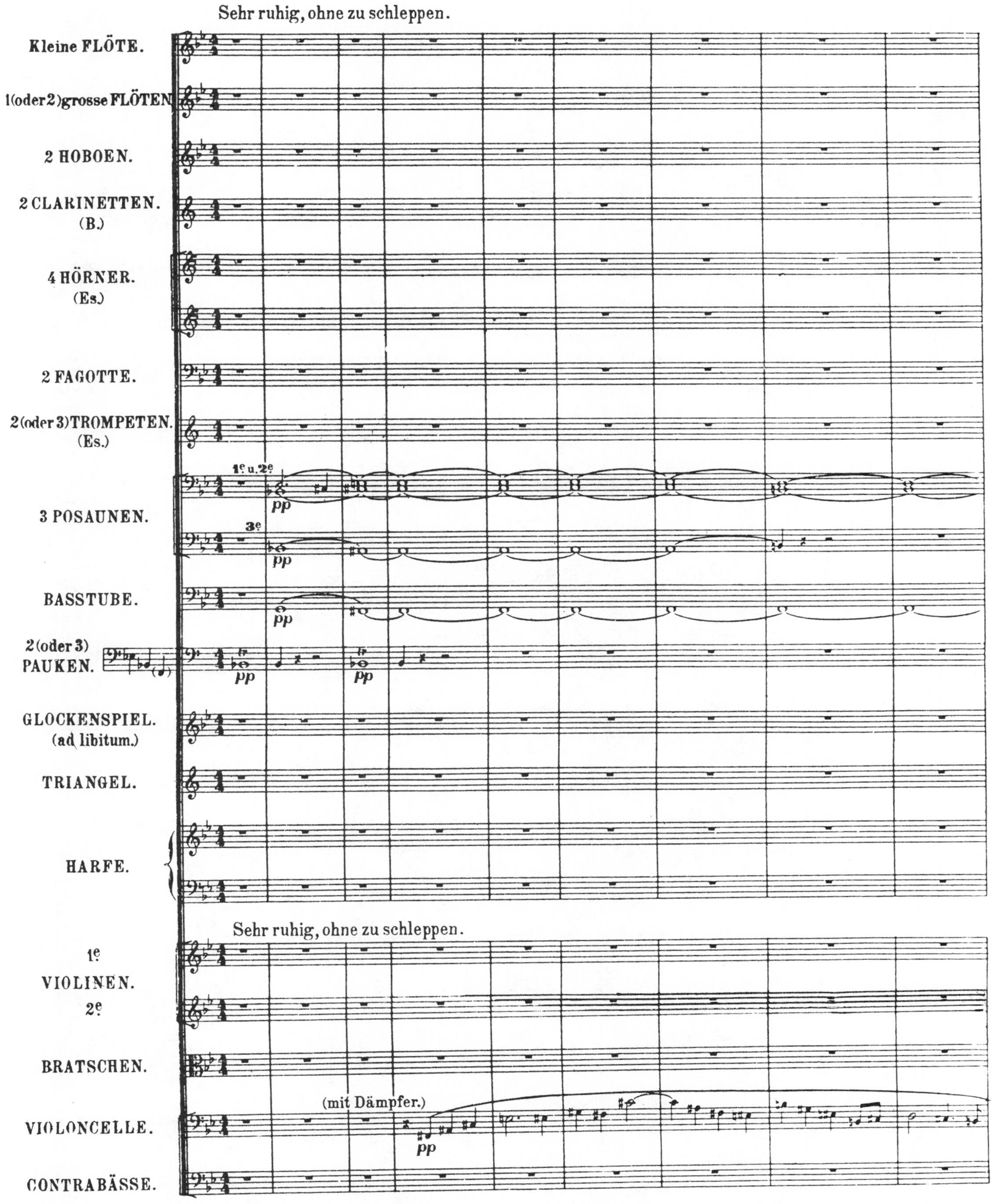
Sehr ruhig, ohne zu schleppen.
Kleine FLÖTE.
1(oder 2) grosse FLÖTEN.
2 HOBOEN.
2 CLARINETTEN. (B.)
4 HÖRNER. (Es.)
2 FAGOTTE.
2 (oder 3) TROMPETEN. (Es.)
1e u. 2e
3 POSAUNEN.
3e
BASSTUBE.
2 (oder 3) PAUKEN.
GLOCKENSPIEL. (ad libitum.)
TRIANGEL.
HARFE.
Sehr ruhig, ohne zu schleppen.
1e
VIOLINEN.
2e
BRATSCHEN.
(mit Dämpfer.)
VIOLONCELLE.
CONTRABÄSSE.

*) *Bei fehlender 3ter Pauke die höhere Octave.*

[In the absence of a third timpani, use the higher octave.]

Siegfried's Funeral Music

"Trauermarsch beim Tode Siegfried's"

from *Götterdämmerung*

(completed 1874)

Siegfried's Funeral Music
INSTRUMENTATION

Piccolo [kl(eine) Fl(öte)]
3 Flutes [gr(osse) Fl(öten)]
3 Oboes [Hob(oen), Hb.]
English Horn [Engl. Hr.]
3 Clarinets [Cl(arinette)]
Bass Clarinet [Bsscl., Bs. Cl.]
3 Bassoons [Fag(otten)]

4 Horns [Hörn(er), Hör.]
3 Trumpets [Tromp(eten), Tr(o)mp., Trp.]
Bass Trumpet [Bsstrmp., Bs. Trp.]
4 Trombones [Pos(aunen)]
2 Tenor Tubas [Tenor-Tuba (Tb.)]
2 Bass Tubas [Bass-Tuba (Tb.)]
Contrabass Tuba [CB. Tub.]

6 Harps [Harfe(n)]

Timpani [Pauken, Pauk.]
  (*2 pairs, 2 players*)

Percussion:
  Triangle [Triangel]
  Cymbals [Becken]
  Tenor Drum [Rührtrommel]

Violins 1, 2 [Viol(inen)]
Violas [Bratschen, Br.]
Cellos [Violoncelle, Vc.]
Basses [Contrabässe, Cb.]

Feierlich.

(Aus dem Rheine sind Nebel aufgestiegen, und erfüllen allmäh-
lich die ganze Bühne, auf welcher der Trauerzug bereits

die Nebel sich wieder, bis endlich die Halle der Gibichungen, wie im ersten Aufzuge, immer erkennbarer hervortritt.—)

END OF EDITION

Dover Piano and Keyboard Editions

ORGAN WORKS, César Franck. Composer's best-known works for organ, including Six Pieces, Trois Pieces, and Trois Chorals. Oblong format for easy use at keyboard. Authoritative Durand edition. 208pp. 11⅜ × 8¼. 25517-4 Pa. **$12.95**

IBERIA AND ESPAÑA: Two Complete Works for Solo Piano, Isaac Albeniz. Spanish composer's greatest piano works in authoritative editions. Includes the popular "Tango". 192pp. 9 × 12. 25367-8 Pa. **$10.95**

GOYESCAS, SPANISH DANCES AND OTHER WORKS FOR SOLO PIANO, Enrique Granados. Great Spanish composer's most admired, most performed suites for the piano, in definitive Spanish editions. 176pp. 9 × 12. 25481-X Pa. **$8.95**

SELECTED PIANO COMPOSITIONS, César Franck, edited by Vincent d'Indy. Outstanding selection of influential French composer's piano works, including early pieces and the two masterpieces—Prelude, Choral and Fugue; and Prelude, Aria and Finale. Ten works in all. 138pp. 9 × 12. 23269-7 Pa. **$10.95**

THE COMPLETE PRELUDES AND ETUDES FOR PIANOFORTE SOLO, Alexander Scriabin. All the preludes and études including many perfectly spun miniatures. Edited by K. N. Igumnov and Y. I. Mil'shteyn. 250pp. 9 × 12. 22919-X Pa. **$10.95**

COMPLETE PIANO SONATAS, Alexander Scriabin. All ten of Scriabin's sonatas, reprinted from an authoritative early Russian edition. 256pp. 8⅜ × 11¼. 25850-5 Pa. **$11.95**

COMPLETE PRELUDES AND ETUDES-TABLEAUX, Serge Rachmaninoff. Forty-one of his greatest works for solo piano, including the riveting C minor, G-minor and B-minor preludes, in authoritative editions. 208pp. 8⅜ × 11¼. 25696-0 Pa. **$10.95**

COMPLETE PIANO SONATAS, Sergei Prokofiev. Definitive Russian edition of nine sonatas (1907–1953), among the most important compositions in the modern piano repertoire. 288pp. 8⅜ × 11¼. (Available in U.S. only) 25689-8 Pa. **$11.95**

GYMNOPÉDIES, GNOSSIENNES AND OTHER WORKS FOR PIANO, Erik Satie. The largest Satie collection of piano works yet published, 17 in all, reprinted from the original French editions. 176pp. 9 × 12. (Not available in France or Germany) 25978-1 Pa. **$9.95**

TWENTY SHORT PIECES FOR PIANO (Sports et Divertissements), Erik Satie. French master's brilliant thumbnail sketches—verbal and musical—of various outdoor sports and amusements. English translations, 20 illustrations. Rare, limited 1925 edition. 48pp. 12 × 8⅞. (Not available in France or Germany) 24365-6 Pa. **$5.95**

COMPLETE PRELUDES, IMPROMPTUS AND VALSES-CAPRICES, Gabriel Fauré. Eighteen elegantly wrought piano works in authoritative editions. Only one-volume collection. 144pp. 9 × 12. (Not available in France or Germany) 25789-4 Pa. **$8.95**

PIANO MUSIC OF BÉLA BARTÓK, Series I, Béla Bartók. New, definitive Archive Edition incorporating composer's corrections. Includes *Funeral March* from *Kossuth, Fourteen Bagatelles,* Bartók's break to modernism. 167pp. 9 × 12. (Available in U.S. only) 24108-4 Pa. **$10.95**

PIANO MUSIC OF BÉLA BARTÓK, Series II, Béla Bartók. Second in the Archie Edition incorporating composer's corrections. 85 short pieces *For Children, Two Elegies, Two Rumanian Dances,* etc. 192pp. 9 × 12. (Available in U.S. only) 24109-2 Pa. **$10.95**

FRENCH PIANO MUSIC, AN ANTHOLOGY, Isidor Phillipp (ed.). 44 complete works, 1670–1905, by Lully, Couperin, Rameau, Alkan, Saint-Saëns, Delibes, Bizet, Godard, many others; favorites, lesser-known examples, but all top quality. 188pp. 9 × 12. (Not available in France or Germany) 23381-2 Pa. **$9.95**

NINETEENTH-CENTURY EUROPEAN PIANO MUSIC: Unfamiliar Masterworks, John Gillespie (ed.). Difficult-to-find études, toccatas, polkas, impromptus, waltzes, etc., by Albéniz, Bizet, Chabrier, Fauré, Smetana, Richard Strauss, Wagner and 16 other composers. 62 pieces. 343pp. 9 × 12. (Not available in France or Germany) 23447-9 Pa. **$15.95**

RARE MASTERPIECES OF RUSSIAN PIANO MUSIC: Eleven Pieces by Glinka, Balakirev, Glazunov and Others, edited by Dmitry Feofanov. Glinka's *Prayer,* Balakirev's *Reverie,* Liapunov's *Transcendental Etude, Op. 11, No. 10,* and eight others—full, authoritative scores from Russian texts. 144pp. 9 × 12. 24659-0 Pa. **$8.95**

HUMORESQUES AND OTHER WORKS FOR SOLO PIANO, Antonin Dvořák. Humoresques, Op. 101, complete, Silhouettes, Op. 8, Poetic Tone Pictures, Theme with Variations, Op. 36, 4 Slavonic Dances, more. 160pp. 9 × 12. 28355-0 Pa. **$9.95**

PIANO MUSIC, Louis M. Gottschalk. 26 pieces (including covers) by early 19th-century American genius. "Bamboula," "The Banjo," other Creole, Negro-based material, through elegant salon music. 301pp. 9¼ × 12. 21683-7 Pa. **$13.95**

SOUSA'S GREAT MARCHES IN PIANO TRANSCRIPTION, John Philip Sousa. Playing edition includes: "The Stars and Stripes Forever," "King Cotton," "Washington Post," much more. 24 illustrations. 111pp. 9 × 12. 23132-1 Pa. **$7.95**

COMPLETE PIANO RAGS, Scott Joplin. All 38 piano rags by the acknowledged master of the form, reprinted from the publisher's original editions complete with sheet music covers. Introduction by David A. Jasen. 208pp. 9 × 12. 25807-6 Pa. **$9.95**

RAGTIME REDISCOVERIES, selected by Trebor Jay Tichenor. 64 unusual rags demonstrate diversity of style, local tradition. Original sheet music. 320pp. 9 × 12. 23776-1 Pa. **$14.95**

RAGTIME RARITIES, edited by Trebor J. Tichenor. 63 tuneful, rediscovered piano rags by 51 composers (or teams). Does not duplicate selections in *Classic Piano Rags* (Dover, 20469-3). 305pp. 9 × 12. 23157-7 Pa. **$12.95**

CLASSIC PIANO RAGS, selected with an introduction by Rudi Blesh. Best ragtime music (1897–1922) by Scott Joplin, James Scott, Joseph F. Lamb, Tom Turpin, nine others. 364pp. 9 × 12. 20469-3 Pa. **$14.95**

RAGTIME GEMS: Original Sheet Music for 25 Ragtime Classics, edited by David A. Jasen. Includes original sheet music and covers for 25 rags, including three of Scott Joplin's finest: *Searchlight Rag, Rose Leaf Rag* and *Fig Leaf Rag.* 122pp. 9 × 12. 25248-5 Pa. **$7.95**

NOCTURNES AND BARCAROLLES FOR SOLO PIANO, Gabriel Fauré. 12 nocturnes and 12 barcarolles reprinted from authoritative French editions. 208pp. 9⅜ × 12¼. (Not available in France or Germany) 27955-3 Pa. **$10.95**

PRELUDES AND FUGUES FOR PIANO, Dmitry Shostakovich. 24 Preludes, Op. 34 and 24 Preludes and Fugues, Op. 87. Reprint of Gosudarstvennoe Izdatel'stvo Muzyka, Moscow, ed. 288pp. 8⅜ × 11. (Available in U.S. only) 26861-6 Pa. **$12.95**

FAVORITE WALTZES, POLKAS AND OTHER DANCES FOR SOLO PIANO, Johann Strauss, Jr. Blue Danube, Tales from Vienna Woods, many other best-known waltzes and other dances. 160pp. 9 × 12. 27851-4 Pa. **$10.95**

SELECTED PIANO WORKS FOR FOUR HANDS, Franz Schubert. 24 separate pieces (16 most popular titles): Three Military Marches, Lebensstürme, Four Polonaises, Four Ländler, etc. Rehearsal numbers added. 273pp. 9 × 12. 23529-7 Pa. **$12.95**

---

*Available from your music dealer or write for **free** Music Catalog to*
Dover Publications, Inc., Dept. MUBI, 31 East 2nd Street, Mineola, N.Y. 11501.

Dover Orchestral Scores

THE SIX BRANDENBURG CONCERTOS AND THE FOUR ORCHESTRAL SUITES IN FULL SCORE, Johann Sebastian Bach. Complete standard Bach-Gesellschaft editions in large, clear format. Study score. 273pp. 9 × 12. 23376-6 Pa. **$11.95**

COMPLETE CONCERTI FOR SOLO KEYBOARD AND ORCHESTRA IN FULL SCORE, Johann Sebastian Bach. Bach's seven complete concerti for solo keyboard and orchestra in full score from the authoritative Bach-Gesellschaft edition. 206pp. 9 × 12. 24929-8 Pa. **$10.95**

THE THREE VIOLIN CONCERTI IN FULL SCORE, Johann Sebastian Bach. Concerto in A Minor, BWV 1041; Concerto in E Major, BWV 1042; and Concerto for Two Violins in D Minor, BWV 1043. Bach-Gesellschaft edition. 64pp. 9⅜ × 12¼. 25124-1 Pa. **$5.95**

GREAT ORGAN CONCERTI, OPP. 4 & 7, IN FULL SCORE, George Frideric Handel. 12 organ concerti composed by great Baroque master are reproduced in full score from the *Deutsche Handelgesellschaft* edition. 138pp. 9⅜ × 12¼. 24462-8 Pa. **$8.95**

COMPLETE CONCERTI GROSSI IN FULL SCORE, George Frideric Handel. Monumental Opus 6 Concerti Grossi, Opus 3 and "Alexander's Feast" Concerti Grossi—19 in all—reproduced from most authoritative edition. 258pp. 9⅜ × 12¼. 24187-4 Pa. **$12.95**

COMPLETE CONCERTI GROSSI IN FULL SCORE, Arcangelo Corelli. All 12 concerti in the famous late nineteenth-century edition prepared by violinist Joseph Joachim and musicologist Friedrich Chrysander. 240pp. 8⅜ × 11¼. 25606-5 Pa. **$12.95**

WATER MUSIC AND MUSIC FOR THE ROYAL FIREWORKS IN FULL SCORE, George Frideric Handel. Full scores of two of the most popular Baroque orchestral works performed today—reprinted from definitive Deutsche Handelgesellschaft edition. Total of 96pp. 8⅜ × 11. 25070-9 Pa. **$6.95**

LATER SYMPHONIES, Wolfgang A. Mozart. Full orchestral scores to last symphonies (Nos. 35–41) reproduced from definitive Breitkopf & Härtel Complete Works edition. Study score. 285pp. 9 × 12. 23052-X Pa. **$11.95**

17 DIVERTIMENTI FOR VARIOUS INSTRUMENTS, Wolfgang A. Mozart. Sparkling pieces of great vitality and brilliance from 1771–1779; consecutively numbered from 1 to 17. Reproduced from definitive Breitkopf & Härtel Complete Works edition. Study score. 241pp. 9⅜ × 12¼. 23862-8 Pa. **$11.95**

PIANO CONCERTOS NOS. 11–16 IN FULL SCORE, Wolfgang Amadeus Mozart. Authoritative Breitkopf & Härtel edition of six staples of the concerto repertoire, including Mozart's cadenzas for Nos. 12–16. 256pp. 9⅜ × 12¼. 25468-2 Pa. **$12.95**

PIANO CONCERTOS NOS. 17–22, Wolfgang Amadeus Mozart. Six complete piano concertos in full score, with Mozart's own cadenzas for Nos. 17–19. Breitkopf & Härtel edition. Study score. 370pp. 9⅜ × 12¼. 23599-8 Pa. **$14.95**

PIANO CONCERTOS NOS. 23–27, Wolfgang Amadeus Mozart. Mozart's last five piano concertos in full score, plus cadenzas for Nos. 23 and 27, and the Concert Rondo in D Major, K.382. Breitkopf & Härtel edition. Study score. 310pp. 9⅜ × 12¼. 23600-5 Pa. **$12.95**

CONCERTI FOR WIND INSTRUMENTS IN FULL SCORE, Wolfgang Amadeus Mozart. Exceptional volume contains ten pieces for orchestra and wind instruments and includes some of Mozart's finest, most popular music. 272pp. 9⅜ × 12¼. 25228-0 Pa. **$13.95**

THE VIOLIN CONCERTI AND THE SINFONIA CONCERTANTE, K.364, IN FULL SCORE, Wolfgang Amadeus Mozart. All five violin concerti and famed double concerto reproduced from authoritative Breitkopf & Härtel Complete Works Edition. 208pp. 9⅜ × 12½. 25169-1 Pa. **$11.95**

SYMPHONIES 88–92 IN FULL SCORE: The Haydn Society Edition, Joseph Haydn. Full score of symphonies Nos. 88 through 92. Large, readable noteheads, ample margins for fingerings, etc., and extensive Editor's Commentary. 304pp. 9 × 12. (Available in U.S. only) 24445-8 Pa. **$13.95**

COMPLETE LONDON SYMPHONIES IN FULL SCORE, Series I and Series II, Joseph Haydn. Reproduced from the Eulenburg editions are Symphonies Nos. 93–98 (Series I) and Nos. 99–104 (Series II). 800pp. 8⅜ × 11¼. (Available in U.S. only) Series I 24982-4 Pa. **$15.95** Series II 24983-2 Pa. **$16.95**

FOUR SYMPHONIES IN FULL SCORE, Franz Schubert. Schubert's four most popular symphonies: No. 4 in C Minor ("Tragic"); No. 5 in B-flat Major; No. 8 in B Minor ("Unfinished"); and No. 9 in C Major ("Great"). Breitkopf & Härtel edition. Study score. 261pp. 9⅜ × 12¼. 23681-1 Pa. **$12.95**

GREAT OVERTURES IN FULL SCORE, Carl Maria von Weber. Overtures to *Oberon, Der Freischutz, Euryanthe* and *Preciosa* reprinted from auhoritative Breitkopf & Härtel editions. 112pp. 9 × 12. 25225-6 Pa. **$8.95**

SYMPHONIES NOS. 1, 2, 3, AND 4 IN FULL SCORE, Ludwig van Beethoven. Republication of H. Litolff edition. 272pp. 9 × 12. 26033-X Pa. **$10.95**

SYMPHONIES NOS. 5, 6 AND 7 IN FULL SCORE, Ludwig van Beethoven. Republication of the H. Litolff edition. 272pp. 9 × 12. 26034-8 Pa. **$10.95**

SYMPHONIES NOS. 8 AND 9 IN FULL SCORE, Ludwig van Beethoven. Republication of the H. Litolff edition. 256pp. 9 × 12. 26035-6 Pa. **$10.95**

SIX GREAT OVERTURES IN FULL SCORE, Ludwig van Beethoven. Six staples of the orchestral repertoire from authoritative Breitkopf & Härtel edition. *Leonore Overtures*, Nos. 1–3; Overtures to *Coriolanus, Egmont, Fidelio.* 288pp. 9 × 12. 24789-9 Pa. **$13.95**

COMPLETE PIANO CONCERTOS IN FULL SCORE, Ludwig van Beethoven. Complete scores of five great Beethoven piano concertos, with all cadenzas as he wrote them, reproduced from authoritative Breitkopf & Härtel edition. New table of contents. 384pp. 9⅜ × 12¼. 24563-2 Pa. **$14.95**

GREAT ROMANTIC VIOLIN CONCERTI IN FULL SCORE, Ludwig van Beethoven, Felix Mendelssohn and Peter Ilyitch Tchaikovsky. The Beethoven Op. 61, Mendelssohn, Op. 64 and Tchaikovsky, Op. 35 concertos reprinted from the Breitkopf & Härtel editions. 224pp. 9 × 12. 24989-1 Pa. **$10.95**

MAJOR ORCHESTRAL WORKS IN FULL SCORE, Felix Mendelssohn. Generally considered to be Mendelssohn's finest orchestral works, here in one volume are: the complete *Midsummer Night's Dream; Hebrides Overture; Calm Sea and Prosperous Voyage Overture;* Symphony No. 3 in A ("Scottish"); and Symphony No. 4 in A ("Italian"). Breitkopf & Härtel edition. Study score. 406pp. 9 × 12. 23184-4 Pa. **$16.95**

COMPLETE SYMPHONIES, Johannes Brahms. Full orchestral scores. No. 1 in C Minor, Op. 68; No. 2 in D Major, Op. 73; No. 3 in F Major, Op. 90; and No. 4 in E Minor, Op. 98. Reproduced from definitive Vienna Gesellschaft der Musikfreunde edition. Study score. 344pp. 9 × 12. 23053-8 Pa. **$13.95**

*Available from your music dealer or write for **free** Music Catalog to*
Dover Publications, Inc., Dept. MUBI, 31 East 2nd Street, Mineola, N.Y. 11501.

Dover Orchestral Scores

THREE ORCHESTRAL WORKS IN FULL SCORE: Academic Festival Overture, Tragic Overture and Variations on a Theme by Joseph Haydn, Johannes Brahms. Reproduced from the authoritative Breitkopf & Härtel edition three of Brahms's great orchestral favorites. Editor's commentary in German and English. 112pp. 9⅜ × 12¼.
24637-X Pa. **$8.95**

COMPLETE CONCERTI IN FULL SCORE, Johannes Brahms. Piano Concertos Nos. 1 and 2; Violin Concerto, Op. 77; Concerto for Violin and Cello, Op. 102. Definitive Breitkopf & Härtel edition. 352pp. 9⅜ × 12¼.
24170-X Pa. **$15.95**

COMPLETE SYMPHONIES IN FULL SCORE, Robert Schumann. No. 1 in B-flat Major, Op. 38 ("Spring"); No. 2 in C Major, Op. 61; No. 3 in E Flat Major, Op. 97 ("Rhenish"); and No. 4 in D Minor, Op. 120. Breitkopf & Härtel editions. Study score. 416pp. 9⅜ × 12¼.
24013-4 Pa. **$17.95**

GREAT WORKS FOR PIANO AND ORCHESTRA IN FULL SCORE, Robert Schumann. Collection of three superb pieces for piano and orchestra, including the popular Piano Concerto in A Minor. Breitkopf & Härtel edition. 183pp. 9⅜ × 12¼.
24340-0 Pa. **$10.95**

THE PIANO CONCERTOS IN FULL SCORE, Frédéric Chopin. The authoritative Breitkopf & Härtel full-score edition in one volume of Piano Concertos No. 1 in E Minor and No. 2 in F Minor. 176pp. 9 × 12.
25835-1 Pa. **$9.95**

THE PIANO CONCERTI IN FULL SCORE, Franz Liszt. Available in one volume the Piano Concerto No. 1 in E-flat Major and the Piano Concerto No. 2 in A Major—are among the most studied, recorded and performed of all works for piano and orchestra. 144pp. 9 × 12.
25221-3 Pa. **$8.95**

SYMPHONY NO. 8 IN G MAJOR, OP. 88, SYMPHONY NO. 9 IN E MINOR, OP. 95 ("NEW WORLD") IN FULL SCORE, Antonín Dvořák. Two celebrated symphonies by the great Czech composer, the Eighth and the immensely popular Ninth, "From the New World" in one volume. 272pp. 9 × 12.
24749-X Pa. **$12.95**

FOUR ORCHESTRAL WORKS IN FULL SCORE: Rapsodie Espagnole, Mother Goose Suite, Valses Nobles et Sentimentales, and Pavane for a Dead Princess, Maurice Ravel. Four of Ravel's most popular orchestral works, reprinted from original full-score French editions. 240pp. 9⅜ × 12¼. (Not available in France or Germany)
25962-5 Pa. **$12.95**

DAPHNIS AND CHLOE IN FULL SCORE, Maurice Ravel. Definitive full-score edition of Ravel's rich musical setting of a Greek fable by Longus is reprinted here from the original French edition. 320pp. 9⅜ × 12¼. (Not available in France or Germany)
25826-2 Pa. **$14.95**

THREE GREAT ORCHESTRAL WORKS IN FULL SCORE, Claude Debussy. Three favorites by influential modernist: *Prélude à l'Après-midi d'un Faune*, *Nocturnes*, and *La Mer*. Reprinted from early French editions. 279pp. 9 × 12.
24441-5 Pa. **$12.95**

SYMPHONY IN D MINOR IN FULL SCORE, César Franck. Superb, authoritative edition of Franck's only symphony, an often-performed and recorded masterwork of late French romantic style. 160pp. 9 × 12.
25373-2 Pa. **$9.95**

THE GREAT WALTZES IN FULL SCORE, Johann Strauss, Jr. Complete scores of eight melodic masterpieces: The Beautiful Blue Danube, Emperor Waltz, Tales of the Vienna Woods, Wiener Blut, four more. Authoritative editions. 336pp. 8⅜ × 11¼.
26009-7 Pa. **$13.95**

FOURTH, FIFTH AND SIXTH SYMPHONIES IN FULL SCORE, Peter Ilyitch Tchaikovsky. Complete orchestral scores of Symphony No. 4 in F minor, Op. 36; Symphony No. 5 in E minor, Op. 64; Symphony No. 6 in B minor, "Pathetique," Op. 74. Study score. Breitkopf & Härtel editions. 480pp. 9⅜ × 12¼.
23861-X Pa. **$19.95**

ROMEO AND JULIET OVERTURE AND CAPRICCIO ITALIEN IN FULL SCORE, Peter Ilyitch Tchaikovsky. Two of Russian master's most popular compositions in high quality, inexpensive reproduction. From authoritative Russian edition. 208pp. 8⅜ × 11½.
25217-5 Pa. **$9.95**

NUTCRACKER SUITE IN FULL SCORE, Peter Ilyitch Tchaikovsky. Among the most popular ballet pieces ever created—a complete, inexpensive, high-quality score to study and enjoy. 128pp. 9 × 12.
25379-1 Pa. **$8.95**

TONE POEMS, SERIES I: DON JUAN, TOD UND VERKLARUNG, and DON QUIXOTE, Richard Strauss. Three of the most often performed and recorded works in entire orchestral repertoire, reproduced in full score from original editions. Study score. 286pp. 9⅜ × 12¼. (Available in U.S. only)
23754-0 Pa. **$13.95**

TONE POEMS, SERIES II: TILL EULENSPIEGELS LUSTIGE STREICHE, ALSO SPRACH ZARATHUSTRA, and EIN HELDENLEBEN, Richard Strauss. Three important orchestral works, including very popular *Till Eulenspiegel's Merry Pranks*, reproduced in full score from original editions. Study score. 315pp. 9⅜ × 12¼. (Available in U.S. only)
23755-9 Pa. **$14.95**

DAS LIED VON DER ERDE IN FULL SCORE, Gustav Mahler. Mahler's masterpiece, a fusion of song and symphony, reprinted from the original 1912 Universal Edition. English translations of song texts. 160pp. 9 × 12.
25657-X Pa. **$8.95**

SYMPHONIES NOS. 1 AND 2 IN FULL SCORE, Gustav Mahler. Unabridged, authoritative Austrian editions of Symphony No. 1 in D Major ("Titan") and Symphony No. 2 in C Minor ("Resurrection"). 384pp. 8½ × 11.
25473-9 Pa. **$14.95**

SYMPHONIES NOS. 3 AND 4 IN FULL SCORE, Gustav Mahler. Two brilliantly contrasting masterworks—one scored for a massive ensemble, the other for small orchestra and soloist—reprinted from authoritative Viennese editions. 368pp. 9⅜ × 12¼. 26166-2 Pa. **$15.95**

SYMPHONY NO. 8 IN FULL SCORE, Gustav Mahler. Superb authoritative edition of massive, complex "Symphony of a Thousand." Scored for orchestra, eight solo voices, double chorus, boys' choir and organ. Reprint of Izdatel'stvo "Muzyka," Moscow, edition. Translation of texts. 272pp. 9⅜ × 12¼. 26022-4 Pa. **$12.95**

THE FIREBIRD IN FULL SCORE (Original 1910 Version), Igor Stravinsky. Handsome, inexpensive edition of modern masterpiece, renowned for brilliant orchestration, glowing color. Authoritative Russian edition. 176pp. 9⅜ × 12¼. (Available in U.S. only)
25535-2 Pa. **$10.95**

PETRUSHKA IN FULL SCORE: Original Version, Igor Stravinsky. The definitive full-score edition of Stravinsky's masterful score for the great Ballets Russes 1911 production of *Petrushka*. 160pp. 9⅜ × 12¼. (Available in U.S. only)
25680-4 Pa. **$9.95**

THE RITE OF SPRING IN FULL SCORE, Igor Stravinsky. A reprint of the original full-score edition of the most famous musical work of the 20th century, created as a ballet score for Diaghilev's Ballets Russes. 176pp. 9⅜ × 12¼. (Available in U.S. only)
25857-2 Pa. **$9.95**

---

*Available from your music dealer or write for **free** Music Catalog to Dover Publications, Inc., Dept. MUBI, 31 East 2nd Street, Mineola, N.Y. 11501.*